SEX

MYLES MUNROE

Pneuma Life Publishing

Copyright © 1999 by Myles Munroe
Sex 101
ISBN 1-56229-127-0

Pneuma Life Publishing
P. O. Box 885
Lanham, Maryland 20703-0885
(301) 577-4052
http://www.pneumalife.com

Printed in the United States of America

INTRODUCTION

While taking the journey towards adulthood, our youth find themselves faced with a constant barrage of conflicting images contrary to the Word of God. Peer pressure, loneliness, movies, music videos, magazines, and even the internet offer little refuge from an all-out attack on their sexual purity. Challenged by day and often tormented by night, young people turn to a church that, at times, has been blamed with failing to "keep it real".

Don't dismay! Dr. Myles Munroe and Dave Burrows have teamed up to offer some very candid and straightforward advice on one of the greatest issues facing our younger generations today—SEX. Young people, there's a very real war being waged for your mind, soul, spirit and body. You don't have to give in, just win!!!! Read and take heed to these words of wisdom, and you'll be victorious over and over again.

Continuing in sexual sin and promiscuity abuses God's grace.

Sexual abstinence is your decision to be in full control of something your body may want to do, but your spirit does not.

The way to purity is to willfully decide to keep yourself pure.

Do not allow yourself to be enticed by empty words, promises, or flattery.

When you are alone together and the moonlight is glistening upon your sweet love's face, it is quite unlikely that a prayer meeting will be taking place.

Refrain from revisiting people or situations that caused you to compromise in the past.

Your conscience is like a warning shot.
If you start running when it sounds,
then you will more than likely win the race.

Sexual sin is a mistake that quickly develops into a habit and eventually ends up leaving you in bondage.

An old trick of the enemy is to get you to believe that out of everyone in love in the world, your love is so strong and your love is so great that you don't have to live by God's Word.

People who willingly persist in sexual sin try to justify their actions by denying God or His judgement exists or claiming that His standards have changed.

You don't have to go around guessing whether or not you are right or wrong. God is your measuring stick. Line up your actions with His Word.

No wed / no bed.
No ring / you get nothing.

Once you cross the line to the point
at which your conscience is blind, then,
dear friend, you've just been grabbed by the
clutches of a reprobate mind.

When you preoccupy yourself with someone's physical or sexual attributes, then you are giving yourself over to lust.

The most satisfying and pleasurable sexual relationships are experienced within the context of marriage.

Don't believe the hype.
Hollywood and friends will always present
you with overblown exaggerations of sex.

The attractions you allow to become distractions cause ungodly actions that leave your salvation in fractions.

When someone comes on to you sexually,
it never means that they think you are
special, but rather
The Special Of The Day.

God will not pick a mate for you —
that would be violating your will to choose.
He may guide and direct you, but you'll
have to pick up His cues.

Being a virtuous woman is as good as it gets, because you are wise enough to abstain from premarital sex.

Part of being a gentleman is respecting the opposite sex. Respecting a woman at all times is a principle you should never neglect.

*Being sexually attracted to someone
is very natural indeed. Acting on those
attractions while you're still single causes
God's heart to be grieved.*

Sex was created by God to express intense feelings for your spouse, not to be played around with like Mickey Mouse.

Sex is beautiful to God and should be to us. For married couples, it's an expression of love, not an expression of lust.

God doesn't condemn singles for having a sexual desire; however, acting on it can place you in danger of hell's fire.

If you think that having sex will automatically cause someone to make a commitment to you, then simply ask the first prostitute you meet about that — she'll tell you that's untrue.

Have you ever been so hungry that it becomes unbearable if you don't eat right away? If you wait, the hunger pangs subside, then, all of a sudden, you're not hungry anymore. Well, all appetites are that way — particularly sexual ones.

*Never go out with a guy who
does not want to come inside
your parent's house.*

Dress like a "ho" and undoubtedly
you will be treated like a "ho".
Contrary to popular belief, what you wear
does determines how much he will care.

You have to be in control of yourself. No one else should be responsible for shouldering the responsibility of your actions.

God will never prevent you from zipping down your pants or taking off your clothes. The decision to utilize self-control at all times is one you must plant firmly in your heart.

Ladies, don't be so quick to go showing off your tail. Don't put your items on display if they are not for sale.

Oftentimes, guys misinterpret affection and sex as being one and the same. Ladies, understand that when you touch him, he's no longer playing games.

When someone loves you, they don't cause you to breech your relationship with God. They support and encourage you in your walk with the Lord and take your commitment to heart.

*The person who is aimless and
has no clear goals or plans in mind,
is someone on whom you cannot afford to
waste your precious time.*

Stay in public places and avoid private spaces on a date. That way you lessen your chances of being the victim of a date rape.

Perhaps you think that when you became born-again, your hormones were replaced by a Christian set. Listen, you need to remember that you still have to keep yourself in check.

If someone does not exhibit the qualities you're looking for in a mate, then why would you choose to spend your time with such a person on a date?

If you think that buying someone's affections causes you to be the one that they will choose, then I hope you'll wake up and smell the coffee before it's only money that you lose.

Love is something that occurs over time, not overnight.

Count the cost before you take your clothes off.
Are you really willing to pay the price?
The consequence of sin is still death, no
matter if you're naughty or nice.

Premarital sex is never free.

Someone always pays in one way or another.

Ladies, everyone knows by now that you don't get something for nothing in this world. If you think someone is buying you things just because "you're so cute", then you're nothing but a silly little girl.

Heavy petting and fondling are not just innocent little games you play. Penetration is not necessary for sperm to enter inside of a woman and cause her to become pregnant.

Those who give in to sexual pressure now, lose out later in life. Those who hold out now win when it counts most.

The most valuable commodity is one that is still unused. The same principle applies to your sexuality.

Animals have sex by instinct.

Humans are supposed to have sex by choice.

Sex and love are very different.
Sex is a desire (appetite).
Love is a decision (commitment).

Sex never causes people to love each other. If sex caused love, then the world would be a very lovely place.

Love should be expressed sexually in the right time and place: marriage.

Love creates feelings, but love is not a feeling. Don't let feelings lead you into believing it is love you are receiving.

True love comes only from the
Author of Love.
All other brands are imitations.

Experience is not the best teacher when it comes to sex. Truth is the best teacher, and the Lord is the most truthful Teacher you will ever find.

The fastest ticket to misery

is to be in a hurry for love.

Sexual stimulation creates an appetite
for more sexual stimulation, which
creates an even greater appetite for sexual
penetration. Don't start anything
you cannot finish righteously.

True friends are people who respect your convictions.

*Always let the opposite sex know
what your convictions are regarding
sex and relationships.*

Listening to "love" songs creates a desire for "love". You need to be careful about what you listen to and what you feed your mind.

Most of the messages in the media today about love are actually messages about lust.

Learn to make friends, not lovers.

Love is caring and patient.
Be careful of impatient love.

There is no school for love and relationships; you have to educate yourself before you enter in rather than hoping to get on-the-job training.

If you have failed sexually, that does not mean you have to keep failing.

Styles and fashions change but standards remain the same. There is nothing wrong with fashion as long as it does not compromise your standards.

Where purpose is not known, abuse is inevitable. The more you know about the purpose of sex, the less likely you are to abuse it.

A good time is just that, a good period of time. If that's all someone is looking for with you, then that person is as good as slime.

Condoms can sometimes be characterized as "con" jobs into being "dumb".

There is no such thing as safe sex.
Sex can be made safer with certain precautions,
but there are always risks involved.
The safest sex is no sex.

Peer pressure is just a weapon attacking the quality of your future. It will always be more important to get an education and develop yourself rather than conforming to win another's approval.

Self control means you have to control yourself,
not leave it up to someone else.

The only thing wrong with being a virgin is that there aren't enough people who were smart enough to make such a wise choice.

Flirting and teasing are open invitations for trouble. Say what you mean and mean what you say.

Many guys misinterpret a young lady's desire to have a relationship as an open invitation to have sex. Make sure you are clear about your sexual convictions so that such confusion is put in check.

Many young ladies misinterpret the attention a guy pays as his wanting to have a relationship, when many times he's just planning ways to get up under your slip.

Sex outside of marriage leaves a long trail of consequences, which often include broken homes and broken hearts, unplanned pregnancies and abortion, welfare and a lower quality of life, STD'S and AIDS.

Since God invented sex, then who could possibly know better than He how it should operate?

God sets rules for your ultimate enjoyment so that you can avoid ultimate pain.

Teenagers are among the largest and fastest growing groups carrying STD'S and the AIDS virus. Remember that fact when you are thinking someone is just "too nice" or "too young" to hand you what could be your death permit.

It does not make any more sense
to have sex with someone you do not
know than it would to let a stranger have
open access to your bank account.
Keep your valuable sprotected.

*Going out in groups removes
a lot of pressure to put yourself in
compromising situations.*

Masturbation and pornography are like many other habits — easy to get into and hard to break.

Homosexuality is abnormal.
It is never normal to enter exits.

The later the time of night, the more you risk not doing something right.

Always put a time limit on a date.
Decide beforehand the time that it should begin,
and the time that it will end.

You must respect and love yourself
and know that you alone are complete.
If you think that someone else can make you whole,
then you're setting yourself up for defeat.

If you want your body to be a gift
to the one who will be your lifelong mate,
then don't unwrap it each and every time
you go out on a date.

Single people belong to God.
Touching someone you are not married to
is trespassing on God's property.

When you present your body
to the Lord as a living sacrifice
available for His use, then you will
save your body from many problems
which result from sexual misuse.

*If you have failed in some area,
repent and turn away from your sin.
If you don't then you'll only stay to
fail again and again.*

*Young men, don't allow
yourselves to be entangled in the web of
flattery spun from a promiscuous woman's lips.
What first seems sweet, may leave you weak
and cause your salvation to slip.*

Those who go in search of sexual conquest after sexual conquest will be conquered by the foolishness of their ways. In years to come they will surely regret how they squandered away their days.

Sexiness is something that exudes from within, not from showing off your scantily clad skin.

Sex after marriage was designed to be the icing on the cake. Premarital sex, on the other hand, is nothing but a mistake.

The Bible speaks very plainly and openly about all kinds of sexual issues. Read it and understand its purpose so that it doesn't become something you abuse.

Sexual instincts are common to every animal, but God designed you with a brain and a conscience to not act so instinctively.

Your sex drive is a normal part of you and that cannot be denied. Giving in to its urges and having premarital sex is what must be defied.

When you experience sex with your spouse, it is sex free of condemnation and full of unadulterated pleasure.

No temptation is ever so strong that you will not have a way of escape. Make the right choice when your way is clear before it becomes too late.

Young people, you too are witnesses for Christ, and must practice what you preach. Your example of sexual abstinence is what shall cause many in your generation to be reached.

When it comes to premarital sex and your salvation, you have to know whose commandments you'll keep. Will you experience the joy of victory or suffer the agony of defeat?

Young ladies, you have to be on the lookout for

Dr. Jekyl and Mr. Hyde...

the one who seems so great at first,

but really is just full of jive.

People who truly love you don't use pressure so that you can give them pleasure.

Tactic: "If you love me, then you'll do it."

Response: "If you did love me, you wouldn't ask or pressure me."

Sex is not a treasured experience for most males, this you can take as fact. For most men, their commitment to you only lasts as long as the sexual act.

Drugs and alcohol are prescriptions for sexual compromise. Anything that numbs your logical thinking process should always be despised.

K—i—s—s—i—n—g,
has been scientifically proven
to spread the AIDS virus.

Make investments in your mind,
for beauty fades over time.

Self-control means that you take on the responsibility to not respond.

Infatuation leads to expectations made without the realization that you are acting out a creation from a figment of your imagination.

Ladies, protect your virginity
and keep your hymen in tact.
Gentlemen, be man enough to be a virgin
and wait for marriage to enjoy sexual acts.

Many people will make empty promises to you just to get inside your pants. You have got to guard your heart, maintain your virginity, and not leave it up to chance.

Sex has nothing to do with love.
It is 100% choice.

You can get pregnant or impregnate someone on your very first sexual experience. Don't be like so many others who never once considered its many consequences.

Love is patient and love is kind and does not diminish over time.

If your love is lost because you wait,

then thank God you found out

before it was too late.

*If you don't keep your body in check,
then don't expect that of the opposite sex.*

If you want the kind of relationships found only in soap operas, then your relationships will never last because they're only full of drama.

Just because you "don't get down on the first night," doesn't mean that the second date will all of a sudden make it right.

When you have failed in your sexual life,
condemnation brings on guilt and shame.
Listen, you don't have to be ashamed,
all you have to do is change.

*Someone who really loves you
will support all of your convictions.
Rather than coercing you into having sex,
they will encourage your godly decision.*

Men, a promiscuous woman should be avoided at all costs.

Someone who truly loves you always wants the best for you. Having premarital sex will not give you God's best; it will only give you the blues.

When it comes to having sex, your peers should not influence your mind. Many times that is just as ridiculous as letting the blind lead the blind.

The consequences of having premarital
sex are often greater than you realized.
It leaves many with babies, AIDS, STD'S,
and a future that is jeopardized.

Though its true that women can only get pregnant at certain times, they still can get AIDS at anytime.

Mr. Right will always respect you and never keep you out late at night.

Fornication is more than just the act of sexual penetration. It involves all sexual sins performed outside of marriage.

This is one of the oldest tricks in the book:
A young man trying to make a young
lady feel like she is hurting his feelings by
being so "stuck up" because she is
not giving in to his desires.

God does not condemn the homosexual;
He condemns the act.

Drugs have negative effects on your sexual chemistry. For example, marijuana reduces a male's sperm count.

Instead of living from sexual peak to sexual peak, it is the kingdom of God that you should diligently seek.

Spur of the moment decisions are often the most dangerous. Think carefully before you do anything with the opposite sex.

Aggressive young ladies often become victims of their own aggression.

Singles, you must decide to abstain from premarital sex before its too late. Sex is good and sex is great, but sex is best for those who wait.

When you think you're too weak to abstain from sexual sin, look to God to give you strength over and over again.

You do not have to conform to the ways of the world. All you have to do is practically apply God's Word.

*Don't be a lukewarm Christian —
hot for Jesus one minute, then hot
for your date the next.*

Either you're living for
Christ or dying for satan.
There is no in-between.

Never let anyone or anything
cause your relationship with the
Lord to be breached.

Your reputation is important and is a precious commodity. Having a good reputation is better than gold.

The Word of God is full of knowledge about varying topics and issues. Follow It's advice on how to deal with prostitutes: Do not lust in your heart after her beauty or let her captivate you with her eyes, for the prostitute reduces you to a loaf of bread, and the adulteress preys upon your very life. Proverbs *6:25-26* NIV

Young people, God wants you to be happy, just as long as your happiness does not grieve the Holy Spirit.

If he is not your husband, then you do not have any business playing house like you are his spouse.

Don't be misled; remember that you can't ignore God and succeed. A man will always reap exactly what he sows.

Giving in to sexual sin is the easiest route for many. Taking the easiest way out is the reason hell will be filled with "easy" people.

Young men,
drinking and taking drugs are never
excuses for sexual abuse.

They say big things begin with the first step. The first step to the big problem of sexual bondage is pornography and masturbation.

Your body is not your own; it was purchased for a great price. You were bought with the blood of Jesus when He made the ultimate sacrifice.

Do you know that you are only the salt of the earth as long as you keep your savor? One of the quickest ways to lose you savor is by granting sexual favors.

Contrary to popular opinion,
the Lord should always be your first love.
In your heart, don't forsake Him
by placing Him below, and
placing someone else above.

The Bible plainly states
only the marriage bed that is undefiled.
Sex in any other bed is defiled.

Being in love

is not the reason to experience sex

outside of its season – marriage.

Virtuous women possess a
rarity that is likened to a priceless treasure.
Don't cheapen yourself by being a common object,
only good for sexual pleasures.

Young men, the Bible clearly warns you about the traps of promiscuous women. "Keeping you from the immoral woman, from the smooth tongue of the wayward wife. Do not lust in your heart after her beauty or let her captivate you with her eyes."

Proverbs 6:24-25 NIV

Young ladies, follow after God first, and He shall grant you with your heart's desire. When you run after men, you end up burning yourself by arousing their sexual fires.

OTHER BOOKS TITLES IN 101 SERIES

WIFE 101
HUSBAND 101
SINGLES 101
WEIGHT LOSS 101
MARRIAGE 101
FRIENDSHIP 101
CHRISTIAN LIFE 101